BIRDS OF PREY RESCUE

BIRDS OF PREY RESCUE

Changing the Future for Endangered Wildlife

PAMELA HICKMAN

FIREFLY BOOKS

A Firefly Book

Published by Firefly Books Ltd. 2006

Copyright © 2006 Pamela Hickman

First printing

PUBLISHER CATALOGUING-IN-PUBLICATION DATA (U.S.)
(Library of Congress Standards)

Hickman, Pamela.
Birds of prey rescue : changing the future for endangered wildlife / Pamela Hickman.
[64] p. : col. photos. ; cm. (Firefly animal rescue)
Includes index.
Summary: Provides details and facts about birds of prey from around the world, their endangerment and a range of conservation programs to save them, including profiles of individual conservationists and birds of prey species.
ISBN-13 978-1-55407-145-6 — ISBN-10 1-55407-145-3
ISBN-13 978-1-55407-144-9 — ISBN-10 1-55407-144-5 (pbk.)
1. Birds of prey—Juvenile literature. 2. Endangered species—Juvenile literature. 3. Wildlife conservation—Juvenile literature.
I. Title. II. Series.
598.9 dc22 QL677.78H69 2006

LIBRARY AND ARCHIVES CANADA CATALOGUING IN PUBLICATION DATA
Hickman, Pamela
Birds of prey rescue : changing the future for endangered wildlife / Pamela Hickman.
(Firefly animal rescue)
Includes index.
ISBN-13 978-1-55407-145-6 — ISBN-10 1-55407-145-3 (bound)
ISBN-13 978-1-55407-144-9 — ISBN-10 1-55407-144-5 (pbk.)
1. Birds of prey--Juvenile literature. 2. Endangered species--Juvenile literature.
3. Wildlife conservation--Juvenile fiction. I. Title. II. Series.
QL677.78.H52 2006   j598.9   C2005-904558-2

Published in the United States by
Firefly Books (U.S.) Inc.
P.O. Box 1338, Ellicott Station
Buffalo, New York 14205

Published in Canada by
Firefly Books Ltd.
66 Leek Crescent
Richmond Hill, Ontario L4B 1H1

Cover and interior design: Kathe Gray/electric pear and Ingrid Paulson

Printed in China

The publisher gratefully acknowledges the financial support for our publishing program by the Canada Council for the Arts, the Ontario Arts Council and the Government of Canada through the Book Publishing Industry Development Program.

TABLE OF CONTENTS

RAPTOR RAPTURE

Eagles have been a symbol of royalty as far back as the ancient Egyptians. The sport of falconry has been practiced in the Middle East since the 8th century B.C. For thousands of years, the power and skill of birds of prey, or raptors, have been respected and admired — and, in some cases, feared and loathed.

^ The falcon on this golden statue was a symbol associated with the famous Egyptian pharaoh, King Tutankhamun. He was discovered in his burial chamber wearing a golden collar in the shape of a falcon.

There are about 420 species of raptor in the world, divided into six major families: New World vultures, including condors; Old World vultures, including hawks, eagles, harriers, ospreys and kites; falcons and caracaras; secretary birds; barn owls; and all other owls.

Raptors are meat-eating birds that are well-equipped to hunt. Their eyesight is up to 10 times as powerful as a human's, and some have ultra-sensitive hearing. Their powerful feet and curved talons, or claws, are ideal for catching and killing prey and carrying it off — a harpy eagle's talons are as big as a grizzly bear's claws. The birds' sharp beaks cut and tear the flesh of their prey, like built-in knives and forks.

Despite their expert hunting skills, many raptor species are endangered or threatened — and it's their food that is killing them. Birds have been accidentally poisoned by pesticides and other chemicals in their prey, and deliberately poisoned with tainted bait. Habitat loss, electrocution on power lines, hunting and a decline in prey have added to their troubles.

There are some success stories. Bald eagles and peregrine falcons were recently rescued from the brink of extinction in North America by the combined efforts of governments, scientists and conservation groups. It took over 30 years. Now these same groups are working to save many more species of raptor. Time will tell if they can meet with the same success.

< The peregrine falcon faced extinction in the 1960s and 1970s. Its comeback is a testimony to the power of conservation and committed individuals.

7

THE STORY SO FAR

In most cases, an adult raptor's only enemy is people. In the 1950s, there was a sudden decline in the populations of several species, including peregrine falcons, bald eagles and ospreys. The pesticide DDT was the problem and has since been restricted in many countries. However, poisoning is still a major threat to birds of prey.

Captive-breeding programs, habitat protection and increased public awareness are showing signs of success. Some raptors have been taken off endangered species lists, but others have been added.

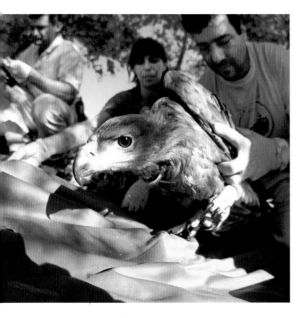

∧ Luis Ferrer checks tagged Spanish imperial eaglets and records their data before releasing them. Monitoring released birds helps researchers understand more about what the birds need to survive in the wild.

1940s The use of many pesticides, including DDT, increases dramatically.

1972 The U.S. restricts the use of DDT. Canada follows suit the next year.

1974 The first captive-bred peregrine falcons are released in Canada.

1982 Scientists count only 22 California condors left in the wild. The last one will be captured in 1987.

1984 The World Center for Birds of Prey opens in Boise, Idaho.

1986 Spain begins an intensive conservation program for the Spanish imperial eagle. The species recovers until 1994, but then declines again.

1987 Operation Burrowing Owl is launched in Saskatchewan.

1988 The Philippine Eagle Foundation is established to develop a plan to save the species.

1992 Reintroduction of California condors begins.

1995 Southern Ontario has its first successful nesting of peregrine falcons in over 30 years.

1995 The burrowing owl is upgraded from threatened to endangered in Canada.

The bald eagle is a symbol of strength and power. Here it wields its huge talons to capture a fish with perfect timing and deadly accuracy.

1997 The Canadian Peregrine Foundation forms in Toronto.

1998 Scientists in India alert people to the crash in local vulture populations.

1999 The peregrine falcon anatum subspecies is removed from the endangered species list in the U.S. and downlisted from endangered to threatened in Canada.

2000 The Oriental white-backed vulture is listed as critically endangered. The Peregrine Fund initiates an emergency Asian Vulture Conservation Program.

2000 The Spanish imperial eagle is officially designated as vulnerable.

2002 Canada passes its Species at Risk Act, which names several species of raptor.

2003 Arizona celebrates the first California condor chick to fledge in the wild since captive breeding began in the 1980s.

2003 The cause of the vulture die-off in India is identified as a common drug used to treat cattle.

2004 The Philippine government protects significantly more Philippine eagle habitat.

2005 India's prime minister calls for a ban on the drug blamed for the country's vulture crisis.

ARMED AND DANGEROUS

Diving through the air at over 185 miles (300 km) per hour, a peregrine falcon delivers a fatal blow to an unwary pigeon. Using its sharp talons, the falcon hooks into the dead bird and carries it off. Soon the prey is plucked and torn into bite-size pieces by the peregrine's sharp, curved beak.

Raptors are built to hunt and kill their prey. They are meat-eaters, and most are at the top of the food chain. This means that they eat animals that have already fed on other animals or plants. The size of the raptor determines what it eats. Ten-inch-tall (25 cm) burrowing owls feed mainly on large insects and can eat their weight in grasshoppers every day. The much larger Philippine eagle prefers bigger prey, such as flying lemurs.

Even the best hunters can't catch food that isn't there, and habitat destruction often leads to fewer prey species. The decline in wild rabbit populations in Spain, due to disease, has had a huge impact on Spanish imperial eagles. When food is not available, breeding slows down or stops and fewer young eagles survive.

Eagles and falcons need large hunting territories to find enough food. A peregrine's hunting range extends more than 15 miles (25 km) from its nest. Philippine eagles need at least 40 square miles (100 km²) of territory. Protecting a raptor's habitat and food supply often leads to the conservation of many other species at the same time.

< Twisting and turning and diving at speeds unmatched by any other bird, a peregrine falcon pursues a pigeon though the air.

POISONED PREY

In the late 1940s, DDT and other chemicals were used to control insect pests in crops and mosquitoes that carried malaria. It turns out they were also killing a lot of other animals, including birds of prey.

The drastic decline in peregrine falcon populations began in North America in the 1950s. The birds were wiped out from large parts of their range, including most of eastern Canada and the U.S. A closer look revealed high levels of pesticides, especially DDT, in the falcons and their eggs.

^ The build-up of DDT in the food chain of many raptors caused their eggs to be weak and brittle. On the left is a healthy peregrine falcon egg, and on the right an egg poisoned by DDT.

Once DDT is in the environment, it doesn't go away — it accumulates in the bodies of the animals that eat it. The insects absorbed the chemicals and were, in turn, eaten by small birds. Since peregrines eat many small birds every day, they consumed high amounts of DDT. And since sick birds are easier to catch than healthy ones, peregrines likely ate a high number of small birds that were suffering from pesticide poisoning.

Although the pesticides didn't kill the adult peregrines, they caused the birds' eggshells to be thinner and more brittle. Eggs easily broke during incubation. The decrease in hatching success meant fewer young survived, and the population declined.

Farmers still spray their crops to control pests and diseases. Hopefully, current safety standards will never allow a poison like DDT to be used again.

The United States and Canada finally restricted the use of DDT in the 1970s, and it's no longer a major factor in the peregrine falcon's survival. However, low breeding numbers, human disturbance and habitat destruction still threaten local populations.

S caling glass walls to perform dangerous rescues and staring down potential attackers sound like superhero stuff, but it's all in a day's work for Maya Basdeo. She coordinates peregrine releases for the Canadian Peregrine Foundation, a Toronto-based organization that's working to help endangered and threatened raptors. There is always a risk of personal injury. "These birds can really hurt people without even intending to."

∧ Maya Basdeo visits a classroom in Belleville, Ontario, to speak about endangered peregrine falcons. It looks like her captive-bred peregrine, Ariel, is doing most of the talking here.

Basdeo's environmental conscience developed early. At age four she was boycotting stores that sold ivory; at nine she was writing letters protesting the wolf cull in British Columbia. "I grew up watching *National Geographic* on TV and wishing I could be the people in those documentaries." Now her dream has come true.

Summer workdays can start at 4:30 a.m. when Basdeo is on a falcon watch. With a team of volunteers, she monitors the flights of newly released peregrine chicks for the first six weeks after they fledge, or begin flying. This is the birds' most critical time. In the wild, 60 percent of peregrines die during these six weeks, when they are perfecting their flying and hunting skills. A further 20 to 30 percent won't reach one year old. But because of Basdeo and other individuals who watch over the young birds, feed them when necessary and rescue them from danger, more peregrines survive each year. Satellite transmitters attached to the young birds help her track them when they fly out of sight. She's recently found that some birds that hatch in Canada end up living in the United States, and vice versa.

The Canadian Peregrine Foundation raptor center raises birds from eggs and then releases them into the wild. Here, Maya Basdeo feeds fresh meat to one of the peregrine chicks under her care.

A safer side of Basdeo's job involves education. She has visited hundreds of classrooms, sharing her love of peregrines, her knowledge of the environment and her vision of a better future. Accompanying her is a live captive-bred peregrine that serves as an ambassador for its species. It seems to be working. "Reaching school groups has made an impact on how students view peregrines, raptors and environmental issues in general."

Basdeo is optimistic about the future of peregrines, but she knows that every generation will need dedicated environmentalists like herself. Her advice? "The most important thing to do is get involved some way, somehow."

KILLING THE COMPETITION

For centuries, raptors have received both good and bad press. They are admired for their hunting skills, strength and agility. But they are also blamed for attacking livestock, cursed by hunters of small game and feared by others.

Predators kill the prey that is easiest to catch—generally the weakest, youngest or oldest. When they kill diseased animals, predators help keep the prey population healthier. In a balanced ecosystem, predators do not cause a population decline in their prey species. Despite their skill, nine out of ten attacks by a raptor are unsuccessful.

Despite their skill, nine out of ten attacks by a raptor are unsuccessful.

If a bird's normal prey is scarce for some reason, it will go after other species, even farm animals. Under normal circumstances though, raptors do not kill a significant number of livestock. Unfortunately, some farmers and ranchers continue to shoot or trap the large birds when they get the chance.

Sometimes anti-predator poisoning campaigns claim unexpected victims. In the United States, endangered California condors have died from eating poisoned bait that was left for coyotes.

Many raptors go after the same animals that people choose to hunt or trap, such as ducks, rabbits, grouse and small fur-bearing animals. Some hunters consider birds of prey to be competition, and they believe that people have more right to kill animals than raptors do. In hunting reserves in Spain, Spanish imperial eagles are deliberately poisoned by hunters. Half of the non-natural eagle deaths between 1995 and 2000 were due to toxic bait, and the number of cases is on the rise. Biologists believe that this poisoning is the main cause of recent eagle population declines.

< A male goshawk raises his deadly talons and prepares to strike a pheasant to the ground.

17

SURVIVAL OF THE CUTEST

The California condor has a wing span of almost 10 feet (3 m) and weighs around 20 pounds (9 kg). The Philippine eagle stands over 3 feet (1 m) tall. These birds and many other large raptors are easy targets for a person with a gun. They sometimes get shot just because they are big, scary or ugly.

∧ The Philippine eagle's wild "hairdo" has attracted many admirers, good and bad. Trophy hunters and collectors valued the eagle's large size and crest of feathers so much that hunting was one of the major causes for the eagle population's collapse.

Beginning in the 1960s, Philippine eagles were hunted and trapped for private collections and zoos. Trophy hunters went after the adults because of their huge size and their long feathers that form a spectacular crest. Young birds were stolen from their nests. Hunting has contributed to the overall decline of the species, from about 6,000 to its present level of 250 birds. Although hunting and trade in Philippine eagles are now against the law, poaching still occurs.

Some people think predators are just vicious killers, not animals that need to hunt in order to survive. If an eagle kills a fawn or an owl carries off a baby rabbit, the raptor is seen as the bad guy. People sometimes kill predators to save the potential victims — it's often a case of "survival of the cutest." Few would disagree that a baby rabbit is cuter than a hawk. But predators play an important role in nature. They help keep prey populations healthy and in balance with their habitat.

The California condor wouldn't win any beauty contests, but that's no reason for letting it become extinct. Thankfully, there are conservationists committed to saving this amazing endangered species.

In a balanced ecosystem, the loss of a few individuals does not usually affect the success of the group. However, when a population is already under stress and is at abnormally low numbers, every loss is serious. The death of breeding-age birds is critical to the survival of the population. So when two California condors were deliberately shot dead in Arizona in 2002, leaving only 74 in the world, there should have been a huge outcry. But the condor, considered ugly by most and "gross" because it is a scavenger, has a hard time gaining public sympathy.

The Philippine eagle is the poster child for conservation in the Philippines. Chosen as the national bird in 1993, it represents the state of its environment: critically endangered. Protecting the eagle's old-growth rainforest home will not only help save the species, but will benefit hundreds of plants and other animals that share the same habitat. A lot is riding on the fate of the eagles.

∧ Feeding and caring for Philippine eaglets is one of the roles of the Philippine Eagle Foundation. This tiny bird will grow dramatically — it belongs to the second largest species of eagle in the world.

Since the 1960s, conservationists have been predicting the Philippine eagle's extinction. The remaining 250 eagles are losing their grip on their forest homes. They are relying on the work of the Philippine Eagle Foundation (PEF) to save them.

In 1987, PEF took charge of the eagles' destiny. It formed a plan and set about bringing the local population on side. The peasant farmers who live in the eagles' remaining habitat often burn a few acres of rainforest to plant crops for their families for a year or two. Once the nutrients in the soil are used up, the farmers move on to burn another plot, and the rainforests are disappearing. Education, compassion and new organic farming methods are slowly changing the way people treat the rainforest and its inhabitants.

PEF's nest reward program also encourages the farmers to become part of the conservation solution. Because the remaining eagles are found in remote forest areas, field biologists need outside help to locate nests. The foundation develops relationships with local people, who monitor the nests and report significant events like the laying of eggs.

In order to discourage poaching, PEF offers a cash reward to anyone who finds and reports a nest. The person is then paid more money throughout the nesting season, as long as the nest remains safe. If the nest is successful and the eagles produce young, a final payment is made. Everyone wins.

Sibagat is one lucky Philippine eagle. It was injured after being caught in a trap, but the Philippine Eagle Foundation rescued it and watched over its recovery and eventual release.

OUT OF BOUNDS

I t's hard enough to protect a species in its nesting territory, but when birds migrate thousands of miles every year, conservation becomes very complicated. Although Canada and the United States have an agreement to protect some birds that cross their border, the treaty does not include birds of prey. When it was signed in 1916, raptors were considered vermin and therefore not worthy of protection. The agreement was updated in 1994, but raptors were not added to the list of protected species.

Birds need food and shelter where they nest, during their migration and where they spend the winter. That's why protecting habitat in one area does not guarantee safety. Around the world, loss of habitat is the biggest threat to endangered species.

Laws that protect wildlife and their habitats can vary a great deal between countries. DDT was restricted in Canada and the U.S. in the early 1970s, but it is still used in Mexico and farther south. Peregrines and other migratory birds are still being exposed to deadly chemicals. In 1995 and 1996, over 20,000 Swainson's hawks — five percent of the world population — died of pesticide poisoning while in their wintering grounds in Argentina. The pesticide responsible for the deaths was banned in Argentina in 1999.

Only about half of adult burrowing owls return to their breeding grounds in Canada each year. Biologists suspect that they are dying either on their migration route or in their wintering habitat in central and coastal Mexico. There are many unanswered questions about what happens to migrating raptors in Latin America. More government-funded research is required to find the answers.

This Swainson's hawk is on top of the world, soaring on its massive wings. Although it is a protected species   >
in its western Canadian habitat, when it migrates to and from South America each year it is vulnerable to all
kinds of dangers.

THE HIGH LIFE

With the exception of burrowing owls, raptors prefer a perch with a view. They choose the highest cliffs or tallest trees within their habitat for nesting. Peregrine falcons even nest on the flat roofs or window ledges of skyscrapers in busy cities. The tall towers serve the same purpose as natural cliffs—they are safe from predators that could attack eggs or young, and they provide a good view of the local prey.

The biggest trees are found in the oldest forests. Unfortunately, these are the same trees that people tend to cut down. Nearly 80 percent of the rainforests in the Philippines have been destroyed since the 1970s. That's bad news for the Philippine eagle, which depends on large areas of dense tropical rainforest for survival.

Spanish imperial eagles once nested in Portugal, Spain and Morocco, but due to widespread destruction of their forest habitat they now breed only in Spain. Even there, most of the old-growth oak forests have been cut down and replanted with commercially valuable species such as pine and eucalyptus. Over half of the surviving eagles are restricted to specially protected areas, such as national parks. Since the eagles require large territories for hunting, the protected areas can only support a limited number of birds. And once the eagles leave the protected areas they are at risk from other dangers, such as electrocution and hunting.

When an eagle loses its forest habitat, hundreds of other species that share the habitat suffer, too. The Peregrine Fund believes that raptor conservation does more than just save specific species. "It can create an umbrella of protection for life's diversity."

< The top of a skyscraper in New York City may seem a strange place to find an endangered peregrine falcon, but scientists have proven that tall buildings are a great substitute for the birds' normal habitat of cliffs or tall trees. Many successful reintroduction programs have started in North America's busiest cities.

Spanish imperial eagles have been on a rollercoaster ride. Quite common in the early 1900s, the species hit a low of only 30 pairs in the 1960s. With an intensive conservation program in Spain in the 1980s, numbers began to climb again until 1994. Since then, the number of eagles has steadily dropped. An estimated 131 pairs remained in 2002, and experts project a decline of more than 26 percent by 2012.

The Spanish Imperial Eagle Action Plan was developed in 1996 by Birdlife International to address the eagles' continuing decline. One of the main threats to Spanish imperial eagles is electrocution on power lines. Each year electrocution kills one percent of the adults and nearly a third of the juvenile eagles. Young eagles find it easier to perch on power line supports. Female juveniles are especially vulnerable to electrocution, since they are heavier and more likely to touch live wires on the perches.

When juveniles leave their nests, they gather in areas where there is lots of food, especially rabbits. Unfortunately, the clearings created by power line construction attract rabbits. Studies prove that more eagles die near power lines where rabbits are abundant.

Even special protected areas cannot guarantee safety. Doñana National Park in Spain is home to one of the largest concentrations of Spanish imperial eagles. Over 125 miles (200 km) of power lines encircle the park and are the major cause of eagle deaths there.

The Action Plan calls for ways to reduce the danger of electrocution. It recommends that new power lines avoid eagle breeding areas and other places where the birds gather. The plan also promotes a new design for electrical pylons that is safe for birds and economical for electric companies. Power lines that run through eagle territories are now being modified, and so far no eagle deaths have been reported in areas where the changes were made.

The huge power lines that cross parts of Spain represent a better life to many citizens but death to a growing number of large birds, including the endangered Spanish imperial eagle. Electrocution on the wires is a major cause of population decline for the eagles, as well as species such as this great bustard.   >

GET THE LEAD OUT

Scavengers are the clean-up crew of the bird world. They use their keen eyesight and excellent sense of smell to zero in on dead animals. Their strong, hooked beaks and sharp talons tear the carcasses into bite-sized bits. And their characteristic bald heads are nature's way of making it easy to wash up after a messy meal. Scavengers like vultures and condors have strong digestive systems, so they can eat rotting meat without getting sick. But their food is killing them anyway.

California condors are dying from eating carcasses that contain lead shot, the pellets that come from the guns of hunters. Animals that have been shot but not retrieved by hunters can die of their wounds and become food for scavengers. In July 2000, four captive-bred condors released into Arizona were found dead as a result of lead poisoning. One of the dead birds had eaten 17 shotgun pellets with its meals. In 2002, 14 wild condors were found with seriously high lead levels.

The following year, biologists in Arizona trapped all the condors in the wild to take blood samples and test for lead. They found 13 cases of lead exposure; five birds required immediate treatment at the Phoenix Zoo. Thankfully, all of the birds survived. Researchers also try to locate carcasses that the condors are feeding on. The dead animals are x-rayed for lead shot. Birds known to feed on carcasses containing lead are then captured and tested for lead poisoning.

Conservationists are urging governments to ban lead shot and make hunters use non-toxic alternatives. Many believe that the fight to save condors can be won if lead in carcasses can be eliminated.

< The Andean condor's strong, hooked beak will make short work of the bloody carcass at its feet. The scavenger is protected from disease by its strong digestive system, but has no defense against lead poisoning from the lead shot used by many hunters.

DOING THE DIRTY WORK

∧ In Mumbai (Bombay), vultures play a vital role in the Parsi religion. When religious members die, their corpses are placed on the Tower of Silence in a "sky burial" ceremony. Vultures gather noisily to dispose of the bodies.

Turning a dead cow into a pile of gleaming bones may not be your idea of a good job, but vultures don't seem to mind—a large flock can clean a carcass in 20 minutes.

Vultures' quick disposal skills get rid of unsightly animal bodies in cities and villages. In India, they are found in large numbers around slaughterhouses, tanneries (where animal hides are made into leather) and garbage dumps. Mills that process bones to be made into tallow and glue first rely on vultures to pick the bones clean. Local farmers also rely on them to eat dead livestock. In the Hindu religion, cows are considered sacred, so they are never killed or eaten. And since Muslims do not eat beef unless the animals have been specially butchered, carcasses are left for the vultures. It's a natural solution to an unpleasant problem. The vultures even help control livestock diseases by eliminating infected animals.

Until recently, the Oriental white-backed vulture was one of the most common large raptors in the world. In 10 years, these birds, along with two other related species, have become critically endangered. The Peregrine Fund, a world leader in raptor research and conservation, now predicts they will be extinct in the wild by 2009.

Until recently, a huge flock of Oriental white-backed vultures polishing off a dead cow was a normal sight in India. But in the past 10 years, these birds have become critically endangered and are headed for extinction.

In April 2003, after two years of studying dead vultures, the reason for the population crashes was discovered. The birds are dying after they eat dead cattle that have been treated with a common drug. The drug causes kidney failure in the birds, and they die quickly. The Peregrine Fund warns that people must act immediately to prevent the species' extinction.

The drastic decline in India's vultures will have a big impact on the communities that rely on these birds for clean-up. Without vultures around, people will have to deal with the labor and expense of disposing of animal carcasses. Fewer vultures means people will be exposed to more dead animals, and this can lead to health problems. In addition, more carcasses lying around will attract other types of scavengers, such as wild dogs, cats and rats. As their populations go up, the risk of diseases such as rabies and plague will also increase.

I n the fall of 2000, Lindsay Oaks, a veterinary microbiologist at Washington State University, flew to Pakistan for the first time. He was on a mission: to find out why thousands of vultures were dying.

^ Veterinary microbiologist Lindsay Oaks led the team of researchers who identified the cause of the vulture population collapse in India, Pakistan and Nepal. He now waits for the local governments to outlaw the drug that is killing the birds.

This was the first time Oaks had seen Old World vultures in their natural habitat, and it was unforgettable. "They may be ungainly and unappealing to many up close or on the ground, but they certainly are lovely to see in the air." Unfortunately, the once-common vultures are rare sights in many parts of India, Pakistan and Nepal today.

The populations of three species of Asian vulture, including the Oriental white-backed vulture, have been in a steep decline since the early 1990s. A virus was the first suspect, but Oaks, an expert on infectious diseases in birds, proved otherwise. The team spent many days in the field collecting tissue samples of dead vultures and analyzing them later in laboratories. It was a slow process. Finally, in 2003, Oaks identified the cause of death: a drug called diclofenac that veterinarians prescribe for sick cattle.

Now that the problem has been identified, what's next? Oaks says that saving the birds requires three things. An immediate ban on the drug is the most obvious first step. India's prime minister called for a ban of veterinary diclofenac in March 2005, but little had changed seven months later. Nepal and Pakistan are talking about doing something but appear unable to take action. "It is hard not to be a bit discouraged."

Second, everyone from government officials to cattle owners must learn how serious the situation is. Each farmer who treats cattle with diclofenac is part of the problem, but also part of the solution.

Third, healthy vultures need to be captured and kept safe. These birds may be used in the future for captive-breeding and release programs once the environment is clear of the drug.

Changing the way people do things takes time, but time is not on the vultures' side. "They have only two to three years left," warns Oaks. Although he has only a small role in the recovery process, he will continue to share his knowledge. "I can help do a lot of nagging if needed."

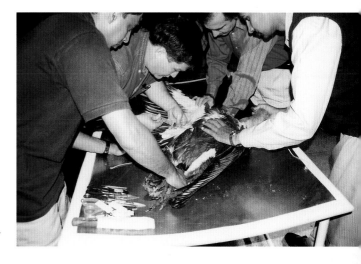

∧ (top) Dr. Oaks and his team work quickly on a dead vulture in their lab. The analysis of tissue samples is key to figuring out what is killing the birds.

(bottom) Dr. Oaks takes samples from a dead vulture found during some field work. It took two years of careful analysis to solve the puzzle of the dramatic collapse in vulture populations.

33

LOW LIFE

The burrowing owl is different from most owl species. It nests underground, is active during the day as well as at night, doesn't mind living near people and eats large insects as well as mice. Unlike other raptors, burrowing owls are not at the top of their food chain. They are preyed upon by hawks, badgers, snakes and other predators.

Burrowing owls live on open prairies. The western burrowing owl, a subspecies, nests in western North America. It has declined throughout its range but most dramatically on the Canadian prairies. The owls are gone from Manitoba and British Columbia, and fewer than 1,000 pairs of burrowing owls remain in southern Saskatchewan and Alberta. That's less than half of the 1988 total.

Farming and other developments have destroyed 75 percent of Canada's original prairies. And within the remaining small area, suitable nesting sites are disappearing. Burrowing owls don't dig their own nests — instead they take over the burrows of other prairie dwellers, mainly ground squirrels. Unfortunately, ground squirrels are considered a major pest in agriculture and they have been exterminated in many areas. Without burrows, the owls have nowhere to nest, shelter from the weather or hide from predators. Burrows are important to their survival during migration, as well. In the Great Plains of central North America, 99 percent of ground squirrel colonies have been destroyed.

Spraying for grasshoppers and other insects reduces the owls' food supply. When food is scarce, fewer young survive. Adults are also more vulnerable to predators when they have to travel further from their burrow and spend more time looking for food.

A major public awareness campaign aimed at landowners in Saskatchewan and Alberta began in 1987. But despite increased protection for the birds, their numbers continue to drop.

Popping out of their underground home, a family of burrowing owls watches for danger before hopping out to find some food. Burrowing owls are hunted by other birds of prey, such as hawks.　　>

When you see a 10-inch-tall (25 cm) owl standing in a pasture full of 1,200-pound (545 kg) cattle, you might worry about the owl's chances of survival. But the owl is actually better off because of the cattle. And many ranchers are the burrowing owl's greatest supporters.

∧ Operation Grasslands Community works with landowners to protect tiny burrowing owls like this one, which was rehabilitated and released in Medicine Hat, Alberta.

Burrowing owls depend on open prairie habitat. They need tall grasses in their hunting grounds near creek beds and wetlands, but shorter grass around their nesting burrows. Long ago, vast herds of bison performed the role of lawn mowers, but that job has been taken over by the large herds of cattle common across the countryside of southern Alberta and Saskatchewan.

Operation Burrowing Owl formed in Saskatchewan in 1987 to teach people about the plight of the endangered owls, and to promote good conservation practices. A similar organization, Operation Grassland Community, formed two years later in Alberta. Together, they bring new meaning to the term "grassroots organization."

More than 700 landowners, volunteers, experts and staff work together to ensure habitat protection for the owls on more than 425,000 acres (170,000 ha) of nesting habitat. Participants quickly learn that a healthy ecosystem benefits not only wildlife, but everyone who depends on the land.

The burrowing owl is a bit bigger than our common American robin. Like the robin, the owl also migrates south during the winter. Researchers have recently discovered major wintering grounds in central and coastal Mexico and southern Texas.

In the past, ranchers went out of their way to exterminate ground squirrels and other burrowing animals. But research has recently suggested that these animals and their burrows pose no real threat to cattle. Now more ranchers are learning to live with a few ground squirrels in their pastures. This, in turn, means more burrows are available for the owls to nest and shelter in.

> The survival and recovery of burrowing owls depends on the protection of their grassland ecosystem, so local landowners and managers are the key to their success. As one wildlife biologist notes, "You can have all the public goodwill, funding and good science that you want, but without landowner co-operation, your recovery plan is dead in the water."

Y ou might think that running 250 cattle over 6,000 acres (2400 ha) of ranch land in southern Alberta would be more than enough to do. But rancher Craig Horner also works on behalf of the endangered burrowing owls that nest on his land.

∧ Rancher Craig Horner is a proud supporter of the Operation Grassland Community program in Alberta.

Horner is part of the Operation Grassland Community (OGC) program. He's one of many ranchers and farmers who are concerned about the decline of several native prairie species, including the "weird little birds" that live in his pasture. For seven years, Horner and his family have hoped that the owls would return from their migration in mid-May. They've had up to four pairs nesting in the past, but in 2003 there were none. "That was very disappointing. The owls have been part of my landscape forever. I'm not really certain what's going on."

How does participating in OGC affect his ranching operation? "It's more about awareness than actually doing things differently," he explains. Since burrowing owls prefer to nest in grazed grassland, they benefit from the presence of Horner's cattle. He's content to let the ground squirrels live out in the pasture, ensuring available burrows for the owls should they return. And he allows biologists on his land to do counts, check nests and monitor any birds they find. Other than that, it's business as usual — except for the time when he was out checking the cows and came across seven burrowing owl chicks standing around their hole, gazing at him. "I sat for a while just watching them," Horner recalls. "It was quite exciting."

The burrowing owl is a good friend to farmers and ranchers. The birds prey on crop-eating pests such as large insects and mice, helping to protect grain fields and pastures in the prairies.

Despite the recent lack of burrowing owls on the ranch, Horner isn't ready to call it quits. "I'm looking long-term." He doesn't know if the birds will return to his ranch or not, but if they do, they will find a hardy welcome and a caring family.

PROTECTIVE PARENTS

Large raptors often mate for life. The adult birds spend a lot of energy protecting their nest and young, and stay around until the juveniles leave the nest and become independent. That's 20 months for Philippine eagles. Because of the time involved in raising their young, many large raptors have a low reproductive rate. California condors produce only one egg every two years; Philippine eagles also nest every second year. The quality of care given their single young greatly improves the chances of survival.

Parental experience plays a major role in successful nesting. Fully mature Spanish imperial eagles nest more successfully than younger ones. And it is common for inexperienced pairs of California condors to have unsuccessful nests in their first couple of tries.

Burrowing owls improve the survival rate of their young by having larger families. Each pair produces a clutch of about seven eggs each spring. This helps the population withstand the loss of young, mainly due to predation. Baby owls even help defend themselves. From the depths of their burrow, the young birds make a sound like a rattlesnake to scare away intruders. It's not always successful—up to half of the eggs and young are killed, mainly by badgers. Even when owlets survive and fledge, many are killed by predators before they have a chance to migrate.

Larger animals tend to live longer and reach sexual maturity later in life than smaller animals. Condors begin breeding at six to eight years old and live up to 60 years. When a breeding-age adult is killed, it is a big setback for the population. It will take at least six years to replace the dead bird with another individual capable of reproducing. Given the species' low reproductive rate, the death rate can easily exceed the birth rate and lead to further population declines. Recovery of these large birds is a very slow process.

This peregrine falcon chick will be well cared for by both parents until it is able to fly on its own after about 40 days. >

SIBLING RIVALRY

Fighting with your brother or sister isn't uncommon, but young Spanish imperial eagles go to extremes. The older of two chicks usually kills its younger sibling within a week or so after hatching. This behavior is called cainism.

A female Spanish imperial eagle usually lays two eggs. One egg tends to be larger than the other and hatches a few days before the smaller one. By the time the second one hatches, the first chick is stronger, larger and more experienced at feeding, so it can easily dominate.

Within the first day or two, the older chick begins attacking the younger. Although the second chick fights back at first, it eventually becomes so intimidated that it stops fighting and feeding. It quickly loses weight and becomes too weak to survive. The mother bird pays more attention to the larger chick and feeds it first. Although she attempts to feed the other chick, too, its lack of response eventually causes her to give up. Plenty of food has been found in the nests of chicks that have died of cainism, so food supply is not a factor in the bird's death.

Cainism is a natural behavior for a number of large eagle species. Under normal circumstances it would not be a major factor leading to population decline. However, since the Spanish imperial eagle population has dropped to critically low levels, mainly as a result of habitat loss and electrocutions, each chick that dies in the nest is a significant blow to the species' survival.

Scientists who raise eagles in captivity have developed a method for doubling the survival rate of chicks. They remove the weaker chick to a different nest that contains young of the same size. The "foster parents" help raise the chick successfully.

< Chances are good that one of these Spanish imperial eaglets will die within a week of hatching. That's because its slightly older, and therefore larger, brother or sister will kill it. This is a natural behavior of several eagle species, but it is frustrating for the conservationists who are trying to increase the eagle's chances for survival.

Sophie Osborn is the Peregrine Fund's field manager for the California Condor Restoration Project in Arizona. One of her jobs is to monitor the love life of released condors. Some of Osborne's field notes read like a soap opera:

∧ It may take another California condor to appreciate the beauty of this bird. Fortunately, some of the newly released condors in Arizona are attracting mates and starting to breed in the wild.

FEBRUARY 5, 2004

Condors 134 and 149, who for the past two years appeared to be a pair, have officially broken up. Condor 134 has yet to bestow his attentions on another female. Condor 149, meanwhile, has been consorting with Condor 114.

One new potential pairing that we are especially excited about is that of Condors 136 and 187. While we are delighted that Condor 136 is finally being appreciated by the males of her species, we are also delighted that Condor 187 has transferred his affections to her. Last year, Condor 187's attentions were focused on Condor 176.

Lined up and numbered like athletes in an Olympic race, these juvenile condors are part of the California Condor Restoration Project in Arizona. Each bird is monitored closely to see what it eats, who it associates with and where it goes.

The world's population of wild California condors plummeted to just 22 in 1982. Desperate times require desperate measures, as they say, so biologists trapped the last wild one in 1987. They brought it to their captive-breeding center where it was kept with the remaining 26 captive condors, safe from the dangers of the "real world." From that point, the survival of the species was dependent on a captive-breeding and release program.

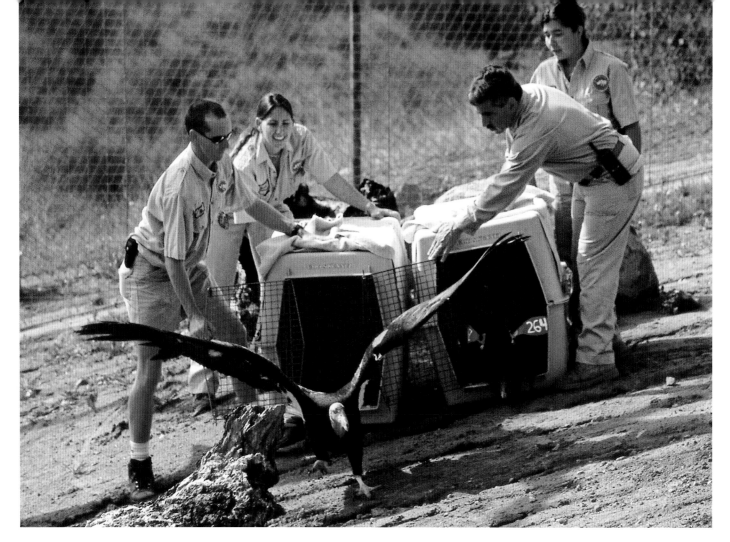

Two female California condors are released into the San Diego Zoo's Wild Animal Park, where biologists will teach newly hatched condor chicks how to behave like condors. When the chicks are old enough, they will be released into the wild.

In 1996, the U.S. Fish and Wildlife Service launched the California Condor Restoration Project, and the Peregrine Fund is in charge of the Arizona portion. The program's aim is to manage the captive-breeding and release of these critically endangered birds so that they can establish a self-sustaining population in the wild. The ultimate goal is to remove them from the endangered species list in the United States.

Since newly released condors don't have parents to teach them about safety, biologists do their best to prepare the young birds for life on the outside. Part of the preparation involves shock treatment. Fake power poles are set up in the captive birds' flight facilities, and the birds receive a small shock if they land on a pole. They rarely land more than twice before they have learned to avoid power poles altogether.

By January 2004, there were 215 California condors in the world, including 90 in the wild. The population has come a long way, and the increase is due almost exclusively to the success of captive breeding. But there's still a lot of work to do. Although wild birds are mating and nesting under Sophie Osborn's watchful eye, few young have survived so far. The year 2003 marked the first time in 23 years that a California condor chick had successfully fledged in the wild in Arizona.

∧ Although wild condors are mating and laying eggs in the wild, few of the eggs or young have survived so far. Here, a U.S. Fish and Wildlife officer removes condor eggs from the wild and replaces them with a condor egg from the San Diego Zoo. The removed eggs will be hatched in the zoo's facility, where their chance of success is much higher.

47

CAPTIVE BREEDING

Peregrine falcons and California condors owe their lives to captive breeders. When the environment became too toxic for these birds, scientists took them in, nursed them back to health and began breeding programs to help build the populations back up. Without captive-bred birds for release, these species would likely be extinct.

Since many large raptors don't reach breeding age for five or more years, there is a long delay between hatching and being able to reproduce. Peregrine falcons, though, breed in their second year. That was a big help when it came to speeding up their recovery.

Captive breeding involves a variety of techniques that are adjusted according to the species. Since some captive birds refuse or are unable to mate, artificial insemination (AI) is a good alternative for biologists to use. Artificial insemination involves collecting sperm from a male and injecting it into a female so she can become pregnant without actually mating. The first Philippine eagle chick conceived through artificial insemination hatched in 1992.

∧ This peregrine falcon chick is the product of a captive-breeding program. In two years, it will be able to breed and help rebuild the population numbers in the wild.

< A rare glimpse of a family of peregrine falcons at the entrance to their nest high up on a sheer cliff. Peregrine falcons have come back from the brink of extinction thanks to the imagination and skill of conservationists who launched an emergency captive breeding and release program that succeeded over a number of decades.

A captive-bred peregrine falcon chick is placed in the nest of a prairie falcon, where it will be raised like one of the family. Using other, related species to help hatch eggs or raise the young of endangered species has proven very successful.

Peregrines are prime candidates for what's called double clutching. When a peregrine nests, she lays two to five eggs. If each egg is removed after it is laid, she will continue to lay more eggs to get to her ideal number. By removing eggs and incubating them artificially, biologists are able to stimulate the mother bird to lay up to twice her normal number of eggs. (This is similar to what farmers do with hens to increase egg production.)

Another way to increase a bird's nesting success is called direct fostering. Falcons that were suffering from DDT poisoning laid thin-shelled eggs that were easily broken during incubation. To avoid destruction of the eggs, biologists removed them from the falcons' nests and hatched them in their labs. Three-week-old baby falcons were exchanged for the eggs so that the adult pairs could rear the young in the wild.

Sometimes eggs need foster care. The endangered South American aplomado falcon owes a lot to its close relative, the peregrine. The eggs of captive aplomado falcons are removed from their nests (stimulating the females to double clutch) and placed under nesting captive peregrines. After a few days the eggs can be transferred to incubators for successful hatching. The peregrines' help greatly increases the chances of chick survival.

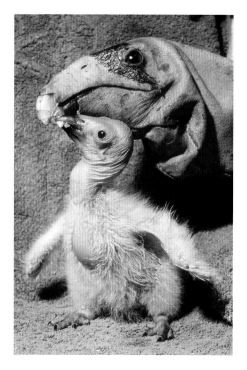

∧ When caring for a baby bird, there is a chance that the chick will think the human caregiver is actually its real mother. This behavior, called imprinting, can spell disaster in the wild if the bird grows up to be unafraid of, or attracted to, humans. One way to avoid this problem is through disguise. Here, a condor chick is being fed by a life-sized condor feeding puppet.

REAL HACKERS

Saving peregrine falcons from extinction is one of conservation's greatest successes. Between 1972 and 1996, Canada's captive-breeding center in Wainright, Alberta, produced over 1,550 young peregrines for release. Combined with a similar program in the United States, the peregrine falcon population grew to an estimated 7,000 breeding pairs across North America by 2000.

∧ A researcher opens the door to the hack box without being seen. Inside, the captive-bred chicks are ready to test their new flight feathers and learn to fly and hunt on their own in the wild.

There are no guarantees of success when raising a chick in captivity and releasing it into the wild. Obviously, the birds must be released into suitable habitat that offers food and shelter. But it's up to their natural instincts to learn to hunt successfully and avoid danger. The job of the breeder is to give the birds the best possible chance for survival. Many raptor breeders rely on an age-old technique known as hacking, originally developed by falconers.

A special hack box is placed on a cliff or, in the case of many peregrines, the top of an office tower. A typical wooden box measures 6 feet wide, 5 feet long and 5 feet deep (1.8 m × 1.5 m × 1.5 m). The box has an indoor space to provide shelter, plus a deck that gives the birds a good view for hunting. Two to four captive-bred chicks are placed in the box when they are a few weeks old. Attendants monitor the young birds and drop food into the box through a tube every day.

These peregrine falcons have returned from hunting to the deck outside their hack box. In a few weeks, they will be able to look after themselves and won't need any more hand-outs. Each bird wears a special tag that enables scientists to track where it goes each day.

The attendants avoid being seen so the birds do not become comfortable around humans. The young birds are not allowed out of the hack box until they are ready to fly, and then the box is opened and they are released. Peregrines have a full set of flight feathers when five to six weeks old. As each day passes, the birds take longer flights away from their box, usually returning in the evening. Their hunting skills gradually improve, and eventually they are able to look after themselves. At that point, the attendants stop feeding them.

Each bird's flights are tracked using satellite transmitters. In several release sites on office towers, cameras are trained on the hack boxes and television monitors in the buildings' lobbies let interested people watch the birds without disturbing them.

The World Center for Birds of Prey in Boise, Idaho, is a jewel in the crown of the Peregrine Fund. It not only houses the group's world headquarters, but is also the heart of the captive-breeding and release programs that are helping sustain wild populations of California condors and aplomado falcons.

There's nothing easy about breeding the world's most endangered raptor species in captivity. How do biologists get the birds to breed? Finding compatible pairs requires a bit of trial and error. Like people, birds are not necessarily attracted to one another. Part of the center's work involves research into the birds' behavior, nutrition and anything else that might improve their health and breeding success during captivity. Artificial insemination is used for some females.

The center is home to about 200 falcons and condors. Its goal is to release enough birds to breed on their own and sustain the populations in the wild. Through its own research, the center is able to support the work of other captive-breeding programs around the world. Sharing its successes and failures is key to helping other projects improve.

∧ (top) The World Centre for Birds of Prey houses some of the world's most endangered raptors. It leads the way in captive-breeding research and shares its knowledge with conservationists around the world.

(bottom) One of the lucky ones. When a chick is hatched and raised in captivity, its chances of living to maturity are greatly increased. The goal is to release it into the wild where it can breed successfully.

Teaching the public, especially youth, about endangered birds of prey is one of the keys to saving species in the future. Here, a staff of The Peregrine Fund and a captive-bred Aplomado falcon engage a young visitor to the World Centre for Birds of Prey.

If the released birds don't survive in the wild, of course, the center will never achieve its goals. That's why it is dedicated to protecting the birds' natural habitats and ensuring their safety once released. Today more than 30,000 children and adults visit the center to learn about the dangers the birds face and what people can do to protect them.

THE FUTURE FOR BIRDS OF PREY

Eagles and other large raptors have appeared on royal coats of arms, coins, flags and weaponry for centuries. Now many appear on endangered species lists around the world.

Although the pesticides that killed so many raptors in the 1950s and 1960s are no longer a serious problem, poisoning from other sources is a major factor in the collapse of Asian vultures and continues to kill California condors.

As their natural habitats shrink in size, so do the populations of birds. And as people move onto the remaining land, power lines go up and pose a serious threat of electrocution, and species such as burrowing owls lose ground to agriculture and the expansion of cities.

The tremendous international success of the recovery programs for peregrine falcons and bald eagles blazed a trail that conservationists, scientists and governments are eager to follow. The captive-breeding centers and the technology that were created to save those species are now being used successfully to save California condors, Philippine eagles and other critically endangered raptors around the world. Governments are protecting more natural habitat, and local people are lending a hand in their own communities.

Raptors are like smoke detectors in your home: they warn us when something is wrong with the health of the environment. We must heed the warning and act quickly.

< The bald eagle won its battle for survival. The challenge now is to rescue a growing list of other endangered birds of prey.

FAST FACTS

Scientific names • about 420 species of birds of prey are divided into six major families: Ciconiidae (New World vultures, including condors), Accipitridae (Old World vultures, including hawks, eagles, harriers, kites), Falconidae (falcons, caracaras), Tytonidae (barn owls), Strigidae (other owls), and Sagittariidae (secretary birds)

Size • range in size from the tiny Bornean falconet that can fit in your hand to the Andean condor, whose wings span 10 feet (3 m)

Life span • small raptors may live up to 5 years; large eagles and condors live 50 or more years

Wings • hawks and owls tend to have short wings that help them fly fast for short distances and easily maneuver through trees
• falcons have long, thin wings for speed; peregrines are the fastest diving
• eagles, vultures and condors have long, broad wings for soaring on air currents

Beaks and Feet • large, sharp, curved beaks for cutting and tearing apart prey
• claw-like talons used for catching and killing prey
• most raptors carry small prey in their talons, but the feet of vultures and condors are too weak

Senses	• very keen eyesight; 8 to 10 times better than humans during the day; owls can see up to 100 times better than humans at night
	• excellent sense of hearing; many owls hunt by hearing alone
	• sense of smell is particularly well developed in vultures
Reproduction	• number of eggs depends on size of species; largest birds tend to lay only one or two eggs, while smaller species lay more
	• owls tend to lay more eggs when food is abundant
	• raptors provide excellent parental care
	• smaller raptors start breeding in their second year, but larger species may wait six to eight years
Diet	• all raptors eat meat
	• the largest raptors feed on the biggest prey: Philippine eagles feed mainly on flying lemurs, Spanish eagles prefer rabbits, and most owls and hawks favor rodents
	• vultures and condors are scavengers that eat carcasses; a vulture eats more than 2 pounds (1 kg) of meat each day

HOW YOU CAN HELP

If you would like to learn more about raptors and the projects designed to protect them, contact the organizations below, or visit their Web sites:

Birdlife International
www.birdlife.net

Wellbrook Court, Girton Road, Cambridge CB3 ONA, United Kingdom
A global partnership of conservation organizations working to protect birds. Web site includes information on thousands of species.

Bombay Natural History Society
www.bnhs.org

Hornbill House, Shaheed Bhagat Singh Road, Mumbai 400 023, India
India's largest non-governmental organization and a leader in the research and recovery of Asian vultures.

Canadian Peregrine Foundation
www.peregrine-foundation.ca

250 Merton Street, Suite 404, Toronto, ON, Canada M4S 1B1
Phone 1-888-709-3944
Provides information on captive breeding and release of peregrines and the Project School Visit program. On the Web site, you can track the movement of tagged peregrines and view webcam images of young peregrines at their hack boxes.

Operation Grassland Community
www.afga.org

Alberta Fish and Game Association, 6924-104 Street, Edmonton, AB, Canada T6H 2L7
Phone (780) 437-2342
Works with farmers and ranchers to preserve prairie habitat and the species that depend on it. Fact sheets, brochures and classroom guide available.

The Peregrine Fund
www.peregrinefund.org

5668 West Flying Hawk Lane, Boise, ID , USA 83709
Phone (208) 362-3716
An excellent source of information on many endangered raptors and
conservation programs around the world. Includes up-to-date news and field
notes from biologists.

Philippine Eagle Foundation
www.philippineeagle.org

VAL Learning Village, Ruby Street, Marfori Heights, Davao City 80,
Philippines
Operates the Classrooms That Make a Difference program, which connects
students in the United States with partners in the Philippines. It also has an
adopt-an-eagle program.

INDEX

PHOTO CREDITS

front cover: Tim Fitzharris/timfitzharris.com
back cover: Y. Galindo/Zoological Society of
        San Diego via Getty Images
p. 2   © Robert McCaw
p. 6   © Robert McCaw
p. 7   © Sandro Vannini/CORBIS/MAGMA
p. 8   Jochem Wijnands/
           picturecontact.com
p. 9   © Daniel J. Cox/CORBIS/MAGMA
p. 10   Jim Zipp/Photoresearchers/
           firstlight.ca
p. 12   © Frans Lanting/Minden Pictures
p. 13   Richard R. Hansen/
           Photoresearchers/firstlight.ca
p. 14   CP/*Belleville Intelligencer*(Darko
           Zeljkovic)
p. 15   Canadian Peregrine Foundation
           (CPF) – www.peregrine-foundation.ca
p. 16   © W. Perry Conway/CORBIS/MAGMA
p. 18   Sonny Tekiko for the Philippine
           Eagle Foundation
p. 19   Mark Newman/Photoresearchers/
           fristlight.ca
p. 20   Anna Mae Sumaya for the
           Philippine Eagle Foundation
p. 21   AFP/Getty Images
p. 23   Jim Zipp/Photoresearchers/
           firstlight.ca
p. 24   Ralph Ginzburg /Alpha Presse
p. 27   Carlos Sanchez Alonso/Oxford
           Scientific
p. 28   © Clive Druett; Papilio/CORBIS/
           MAGMA
p. 30   Alice Schalek/Hulton Archive/Getty
           Images
p. 31   © Geoffrey K. Brown, Ardea London
           Ltd.
p. 32   Courtesy of Lindsay Oaks, DVM,
           PhD, Dip.ACVM
p. 33   (*top and bottom*) Courtesy of Lindsay
           Oaks, DVM, PhD, Dip.ACVM
p. 35   © Jim Brandenburg/Minden
           Pictures
p. 36   CP/Medicine Hat News (Tim Smith)
p. 37   Courtesy of Dr. Gordon Court
p. 38   Courtesy of Craig Horner
p. 39   Courtesy of Dr. Gordon Court
p. 41   © Galen Rowell/CORBIS/MAGMA
p. 42   © W. Perry Conway/CORBIS/MAGMA
p. 44   United States Fish and Wildlife
           Service
p. 45   United States Fish and Wildlife
           Service
p. 46   Y. Galindo/Zoological Society of San
           Diego via Getty Images
p. 47   United States Fish and Wildlife
           Service
p. 48   © DIETMAR NILL/FOTO NATURA/
           Minden Pictures
p. 49   © Frans Lanting/Minden Pictures
p. 50   © Galen Rowell/CORBIS/MAGMA
p. 51   United States Fish and Wildlife
           Service
p. 52   Canadian Peregrine Foundation
           (CPF) – www.peregrine-foundation.ca
p. 53   Canadian Peregrine Foundation
           (CPF) – www.peregrine-foundation.ca
p. 54   (*top and bottom*) Courtesy of the
           World Center for Birds of Prey/The
           Peregrine Fund
p. 55   Courtesy of the World Center for
           Birds of Prey/The Peregrine Fund
p. 56   © W. Perry Conway/CORBIS/MAGMA

AUTHOR'S NOTE

I am grateful to many people for their assistance with the research for this book. In particular, I wish to thank Dr. Lindsay Oaks, Maya Basdeo, Craig Horner, Lindsay Tomyn and Sophie Osborn for sharing their time and expertise with me. I would also like to express my deep appreciation for the work they do on behalf of the world's endangered raptors. Many thanks to my editor Dan Bortolotti, and to Brad Wilson at Firefly.

For Jill.